Rupture and Repair

Jerica Taylor

Advance Praise for *Rupture and Repair*

"In *Rupture and Repair*, Jerica Taylor drops us into the question of 'what to do with the feathers / from the hens / the fox almost catches.' The question centers us in a place of displacement. There's no real footing; even the feathers are ephemeral in their space. And this place of questioning remains throughout the book, enticing with each new configuring of the possible. We are brought gently through bird places, motherhood, the unfamiliar familiar of learning to build family, and the steadied mud of the frog pond. The book unsettles and charms with its depth. Autumn gives way to winter, then early spring but the figuring of the seasons cannot quiet the chorus of animals that guide the pages of *Rupture and Repair*. A fascinating sequence of events and a joy to read."
      —Kari Flickinger, author of *Ceiling Fan*
      and *The Gull and the Bell Tower*

"Taylor's new collection *Rupture and Repair* answers directly to the aching pull of memory and belonging. The exploration, conceived in four parts, charts the rhythm of days, the slightly out of synch, hand in hand with gentle optimism & the wisdom of nature. Taylor's immediacy provides an affirmation of existence, a reminder of what it is to be alive, to survive the winter, and be surrounded by the hope filled continuum of the natural world."
    —Marcelle Newbold, writer & editor

"Knowing when and how to love is more instinct than conditioning. But that requires fearlessness and faith, even when the panic takes over and veils of darkness hide the way forward. Such a journey – a folk heroine's journey – is no small feat and yet, Jerica Taylor travels that route seamlessly for us with a refined gaze and sense of awe for what is possible that is both exhilarating and liberating. *Rupture and Repair* unearths mineralized veins beneath the surface of what we expect from and believe about ourselves and others. The collection is a map that leads us to the *yes* of uncertainty, the *yes* of unbearable loss, the *yes* of courageously uncovering wounds."

—Karen Pierce Gonzalez, author of forthcoming
Coyote in the basket of my rib (Alabaster Leaves)
and publisher, FolkHeart Press

Rupture and Repair

Poems by

Jerica Taylor

Copyright © 2022 Jerica Taylor

All Rights Reserved. This book or any portion thereof may not be reproduced, in whole or in part, in any form (beyond that permitted by Sections 107 and 108 of the U.S Copyright Law and except by reviewers for the public press), without the express written permission of the publisher except for the use of brief quotations in a book review.

Taylor, Jerica / author

Rupture and Repair / Jerica Taylor

Poems

ISBN: 978-1-7365167-8-2

Edited by: Elisabeth Horan
Book Design: Amanda McLeod
Cover Art: Ollie Levy. Used with permission.
Cover Design: Amanda McLeod

PUBLISHER
Animal Heart Press
P.O. Box 322
Thetford Center, Vermont 05075
www.animalheartpress.net

Table of Contents

I. *Hens, Geese, Benedictions*   *11*
    Animate   12
    Some Mornings   13
    Fresh Nectarines   14
    The Five of Us (Are Saving Your Life)   15
    The Blade   17
    POV   18
    Organic Growth   19
    Thermodynamic Equilibrium   20
    October   21

II. *The Answer Is Yes*   *23*
    Simple Ritual   24
    The Lilacs on Lafayette Street   25
    Paquerette   26
    Constance   27
    Sleeping Porch   28
    Saints Peter and Paul   29
    Secret Service   30
    Uncle is Gonna Get You   31
    The Wreck   32

III. *Songs for Waking*   *33*
    Sam Peabody   34
    Tender Cherie   35
    Frost Warning   36
    Reparenting   37
    The Window   38
    Audiation   39
    Honeybells   40
    The Multiverse of the Pond   41

IV. Until We Run Out   *43*

Xylophone   44
13 Thoughts You Had in Rapid Succession When She Walked the Opposite Direction Down the Road   45
10:11   46
Shelterbelt   47
Superstition   48
Mammalian Dive Reflex   49
The Wrong Time to Ask Questions About a Rope Bridge Is When You're In the Middle   50
The Disruption   51
For the Hopeless Scroll Under the Swipe of Your Finger   52

Previous Publications   55
Acknowledgments   56
About the Author   57

I. Hens, Geese, Benedictions

Animate

I never know what to do with the feathers
from the hens
the fox almost catches.

The bird taken leaves behind
a meteor strike
as she explodes from this world.

But the bird that gets free
sheds a trail of gratefulness
and panic.

She preens the near miss.
She must now go bare,
her rump reduced to semiplumes.

I scour the forsythia and the lilac
for buds above the circlet of feathers.
Too early, hard frosts overnight,

but I need hard proof
that we made it back alive
this time, too.

Some Mornings

Some mornings are
geese flying over fast and raucous in the cold November sky.

I want to climb into
the pond and pull the ice up over me like a blanket
and watch their uneven V, urge on the stragglers
and then close my eyes as snow flurries dust my cheeks.

Some evenings are
shallot skin, thin and tough and a struggle to get to the tender heart.

Were I wild with teeth meant for roots
I could bite through it all.

Some evenings are
a pause where the reflections of the ceiling lights are small suns
halved in an unknowable galaxy suspended over my dinner table.

I could reach up and be aflame.

Fresh Nectarines

I long to drown
the way the ant does
sweet promise, tar-slick
gouged cutting board, blue linoleum

How can I go under?

syrup tongue or a mouthful
morbid disappointment
testing the surface tension
an anchor, a drop of joy

The Five of Us (Are Saving Your Life)
after Famous Last Words by My Chemical Romance

5.
I do not know yet what a panic attack is but I am definitely having one. It's a humid summer night, thick with cloud cover. I am in the car with the windows down; it's too much wind but I can't feel enough.

There's a lightning strike coming. My voice is anything but thunder as I scream. I play the song four more times before I pull into my driveway.

4.
It comes at me, furtive, a cat burglar. Chorus and bridge, intro and outro, each undoes a twist in the lock. Furious and bitter and miserable, but also relief and contentment and kindness. In the middle of it all, I recognize myself. I start to remember how to be awake.

3.
The music is turned up and the pit is stirred up and I clutch at my friend, who clutches back at me, as the disconsolate notes that open the song ring through the speakers, through our chests.

In the tender space at the end of the set but before the encore, we are told, if this was the last time we all meet, to keep ourselves alive. I receive it like a benediction, and a promise.

2.

Struggling, hands over my ears, useless against a voice from the inside that I do not know how to make stop.

I'm crying half a line into the bridge. I thought it would be easier to recover, but I am afraid. I say the words over and over, until the emphasis shifts from something I am hearing to something I am declaring. Speaking the way to safety into existence.

1.

There is an outstretched hand, through the ether of this sleepless night. I am sung to through the darkness, over and over, by a song about living at the end of an album about death.

I'll tell you as I am told: survive. Hold on to me; listen with me. Everything you've lived through gets you here, and here, you are alive.

The Blade

I carry a sword inside me, head to hips.

Some evenings, I want to dance until it clangs against my ribs loud enough to be heard.

Outside in the sun in the lingering chill of February, light glints off my chest, blinding. Steel shines just under the skin of my sternum. Is the blade finally going to rend me in half? Or is my body exorcising it like a splinter?

I press my hand to this new breastplate. I do not want to die in the daylight, but I fear turning inward to discover I have been hollowed, and am still walking.

In an unseen future, something could grow in that cleaned-out space; a pruned-back bush dormant for a season, a year, a decade. Any blossom would be an epiphany.

A stem in my hand.

POV

In the story from your point of view, would the paragraphs
be packed with how much you adore me? Would I laugh at
the fool of a character who didn't notice the obvious? Or
would I find in the narrative confirmation of my most bitter
fears? That I am an old chair in an overcrowded room, the tower
of junk piled on me precarious and leaning. You are thinking
about what space would open up if you gave me away
to someone else. All that chair ever really did was hold
the books you had no other place for.

Organic Growth

Cutting back bittersweet is tedious and it has tangled
around the wild rose, married hooks, the couple wound
in mimicry, the twin determination of invasives.

Neither is supposed to grip the rain spout, tickle the louver,
slip tendrils under shingles. Weeds don't care
for what is allowed, and they continue, heedless, upward.

After an hour with the loppers, sore shoulders and aching
calves from tip-toe reaches, I surrender. The bittersweet
can climb my tired limbs, use my sweat-damp forehead as scaffolding.

Let me stretch my frame to accommodate the gentle pressure
of something alive and wanting more. Grow, my hands and your
leaves on the red roof as we settle in for the season.

Thermodynamic Equilibrium

Your hands ache from the cold as soon as the leaves start to change. I always run hot and I hold them when you let me. It is never enough. No matter how much of the heat I transfer, it disperses too quickly, your poor circulation not able to retain the gift. We will never meet in the middle where both the source and the sink are equally comfortable.

October

An oak leaf the size of my sternum, sown
with scarlet sawfly bites, spun sugar milkweed,
deer flattened grass.
October eggplant, shiny black and palm-sized. The pond
is empty on the pendulum swing of vernal.
No frogs sing,
no caddis flies questing to build their prickly home.
The leaves rock
themselves to sleep on the grass above vole tunnels. What a time
to be tender-hearted and afraid. The daisies bloom best
with days of rain.
The kale and mums yearn for the frost. Yellowing birch leaves,
pinecone fingers, hatless acorns, stasis sun, bittersweet berries
wrapped in yellow, a present for the warm weather
to open.

II. The Answer Is Yes

Simple Ritual

There is a simple ritual to contact the dead:

You will need the return address from a card they mailed you though in a pinch your name in their handwriting is enough.

You will need something ugly they gave you that you nevertheless kept.
Intergenerational trauma is best but a curse you still remember in their voice will suffice.

You will need a large orange
and an old birdhouse
and a stained coffee cup.

You won't even need to use any blood if you have a pair of acrylic frame glasses.
Put them on.

You will need to hold the question clearly in your mind. They will not show up for a chat.

If you want to save yourself the time, the answer is usually yes. Were they sorry? Did they mean it? Are they at rest?

Did they love you?

Yes, you look so much like her, wearing those glasses.

The Lilacs on Lafayette Street

I threw myself to the ground when we moved
away from the twins who were my best friends,
and Mrs. Levesque's colossal lilacs.

I could tell the identical girls apart by their crooked mouths.
A mistake of perspective; the lilacs couldn't hide me.

I pressed my cheek to a hundred purple petals,
and cried into the house dresses of the French ladies
next door. *Les sœurs, aussi*, they said,

though they weren't related. I see now who they were;
gardeners of the same soil I would come to be rooted in.

Paquerette

I wonder if this is how you thought your life would go:

Forced to quit smoking cold turkey when you were no longer able to buy the contraband. We knew all along. You had one daughter and three sons who had three sons and one daughter. Two moved away; one came back when her husband died. The other died a husband with three sons.

I wonder about your boss:

Everyone said you were his best, his favorite. He famously dropped money in your name, sent gifts, even paid the bill for your husband's funeral reception. I wonder exactly how he loved you and whether he was inordinately kind, or a stalker.

I wonder when you noticed:

You left the door unlocked. You fed me even when I did not know I was empty. You kept offering, quietly, consistently even though I had been told not to accept that which I hadn't earned.

I wonder about your secret name:

Every return address included your middle initial. I was thirty before I knew the P stood for Paquerette. Daisy. How you must have been admired somewhere before I knew you, bright as the face of a flower.

I wonder when I can see your grave:

Once it's safe to cross state lines, I will visit it alone. I will remember your sly smile when my daughter's school picture was given the center spot on the fridge because, like me, you always loved the girls best.

Constance

The sharp scene of pine needles and warm water washing sand off my feet.

Counting the sand dollars we collected as I traced the varicose veins through your papery skin.

Swim suit and beach towel hung on the suspended rope between trees.

You smoked cigarette after cigarette, ate aspirin like candy, smeared fingerprints on glasses too big for your face. They would be fashionable now. You had them for years, because you only visited the doctor when you were sick and even then it was too late.

I bring my daughter to the ocean, and the same waves pull at her ankles. She has the middle name of my wife's grandmother because yours felt too formal, and I missed you too much.

I hold her hand as you held mine and we wade into the water, eyes down, scanning for treasures of empty shells, the tide a constant pull.

Sleeping Porch

On the street-side of the house
There is a room of windows
that smell of metal and rain

Under the sills is a fold-away couch
Made up with line-dried sheets

This is as close to being asleep as you're going to get
On a night like this

Her mother had said the best of the old houses
All had the sleeping porch
The night cooler outside
Than the inside of the house that had baked all day
In southern exposure under a flat roof

She finishes the dishes, sets the meat to marinate
Overnight, preps the coffee maker and batter
For high-peaked muffins
In the oven before anyone else is even awake

In her housedress and barefoot
Shuts the lights of the kitchen, the bathroom,
The hall. Sets a glass of water on the coaster

Sprawls on top of the covers
Taking up more space than she has ever been willing to
Closes her eyes in the dark
And lets the night bring her down
Degree by degree

Saints Peter and Paul

My mother refuses to attend her own mother's funeral, and I am pressured not to go as well. In a rare and terrifying act of defiance, I go anyway. The chapel is freezing. We are the first funeral of the day and the heat hasn't had the time to warm the cavernous grey marble. Even the wood of the pews is cold under my wool skirt.

There will be consequences when I get home. I loved my grandmother even when my mother wished I would not. A cousin I barely remember gives the eulogy. One of the hymns is in French, and I cry so hard I can't breathe. My father's mother, who sits beside me, rarely initiates touch, but she grips my hand with her ice-cold fingers.

Secret Service

There is a girl in a Nissan Stanza in the J.C. Penney parking lot. The car is idling and she is being yelled at by the driver, who is nearly identical to what she will look like in twenty years, right down to the moles on her neck. On her right is a snow bank, piled high from the slush of the loop road around the mall. There is an urban legend passed around about a homeless man being plowed in. At the summit of the mountain, a twisted shopping cart peeks out. She does not think of broken limbs.

The president came to visit her elementary school on the first day of sixth grade. She was wearing a tunic with tiny maroon flowers and matching stirrup leggings. On the playground for morning recess, students stood under the play structure, gazing up at gunmen in black on the roof of the single-story building. The girl had coughed too loudly in the car on the way to drop-off and was told to stop faking. She was certain if the black-clad men saw her face, they would be ordered to shoot.

The radio in the budget-model car in the frost-heave pocked parking lot is reporting on traffic but there is no traffic nearby, not for at least 50 miles. No one even parks in the next spot. She imagines someone might, and the piercing gaze of a stranger might stop the furious rant. To the no one outside in the grey afternoon, her mother could be singing, mouth open wide.

Uncle is Gonna Get You

Kids should remember birthdays more vividly than they remember the crumble of instant coffee granules finger-sifted into the sugar.

More clearly than they remember the timber of their uncle's voice, the twitch of his moustache and his furious red cheeks as he yelled at them for not making decaf coffee for their grandparents. Kids should be proud of being given responsibility, finally old enough to boil water in the whistling kettle on the electric stove. They should not be screamed at about avoiding caffeine for heart health because they don't understand and they are eight.

They should remember the bitter lick of the spoon, the drip of half and half, more sharply than the voices that reverberated through the house long after everyone had gone home. They should put on the Gloria Estefan cassette and spin circles in the living room as Missile Defence loads on the Sega. They should have their gun ready.

The Wreck

I thought
it would
be easy
to keep
myself
alive.

III. Songs for Waking

Sam Peabody

His name rings out, over the idling of the car,
a flute in a symphony of sky above me.
Someone's mundane business conducted in song,
and I don't have to do anything but listen.

Have you ever called out
with the confidence of a tiny brown bird
wearing yellow jewels like buttercups?
Have you ever been held by the trees?

In this moment, I am loved the way
the white-throated sparrow is loved; for existing.
For its song, no matter how many times it needs to sing
the same notes over and over. I am heard.

Tender Cherie

My eyes go uneven
when the headaches are bad.
One droops and you can tell
as soon as you look at me
what I need. I'm so overstimulated
I can hear the depression of the keys
before the note. Time and perception
go woolly with pain. You start to play
the sweetest song, wide sweeps of melody
recalling a town we've never visited.
I can't speak the title, aphasia setting in.
I say 'cherie,' somehow both the song
and my affection. Your huff of a laugh is
a held note, the soft thunk of the foot pedal.

Frost Warning

March's open palm
slapped the pond with thin, clear ice.
The day before, the spring air was thick with
croaks and calls from the awakened wood frogs.

A scold for indulging in such joy.
The absence of their song is crushing
until I see a frog swim below
and disappear into the muck on the bottom.

Not everything is lost
with one cold night.

With the sting still on your cheek
Tuck yourself under the blankets
as the frogs swaddle themselves in
purple and brown leaves

and when you're ready
when the sun shines
warm enough to melt the brittle glass between
come up for air and sing again.

Reparenting

The things that remain fantasy out of fear
are hydrangeas gone brown from too little rain before they finish
blooming; beautiful and shriveled, existing cheek to cheek.

The gesture that is held back
is the tight curl of a fern that doesn't have time to open before the frost;
hard to look at too closely without mourning.

Someone taught you
that what you love will be taken from you because you love it.
If you loved less,
if you needed less,
you might be granted a cup of soil
for your pale and fragile germination to rest in.

You thirst, ache for the yellow rays through clouds;
surely it is only a matter of hours until you are cut down
by the dark.

Imagine the possibility of a garden:
more room than you could ever need to grow.
You are waiting to open. You have been waiting a very long time.

The Window

My desk bows low to accept the blessing of late afternoon. The high yellow ceilings a temple to the sun, the cat in the rhombus of light a spirit guide.

Mine, mine, mine. There's a hole in my bag of flour and I leave a fine cloud of dust in my wake, and I can never, never stay filled to the top.

No, a winter's sleep is not a grain's death.

I never was much of a stargazer, the window in that place I was trapped taken up with my reflection and the burn of the streetlight.

Once, I taped a note, facing out, for only the driveway to see. "Yes I am."

When the sun falls below the treeline, my room is still warm and yellow. The cat is still flicking his tail across the keyboard.

I can be a small creature of joy or a fractaling of over-treaded paths, but at some point, I always recognize that I have been there before.

Tonight, when the stars come out, I will close the chickens' coop windows and kiss their complaining heads goodnight with the headcount of my flashlight. I will pause under the wild rose, still purple and mostly bare, and listen for the owl ordering dinner. I will apologize to the thorns that catch on my sleeve.

I am the observer in the driveway, looking up at the black ballpoint and the fingerprint on the tape. The girl may not recognize me, if she could see me at all through the glare of her desk lamp, in profile with her ear pressed to the speakers. But I am there as assuredly as we are here, and I see her sign.

Yes, you are. You do. You live.

Audiation

I almost buy a keyboard on Friday morning;
a digital one with weighted keys that serves up
sound like a real piano, for the sole satisfaction
of learning to play a song stuck on repeat in my head.
When I was small, I could copy a tune
I'd only heard once. My parents hoped it meant
I was gifted and hired a tutor. The fluttery sheets
of music made me tense. It soothed me to pick
out on the cracked keys what rumbled inside.
I recall with a spread palm the stretch
of my pinkies and thumbs to reach the farthest
keys and the confusion when a six year old outplayed
me right before I quit. I thought you were good
or you weren't, you had the skill or you didn't,
and sitting on that unbalanced scale left me
perpetually hungry. I have swung too wildly
to the opposite amplitude, denial to overindulgence,
for what I was not allowed then and wish to feed
myself now. Impulsively, I click Add to Cart
on an instrument meant for musicians and not sad
little grown up girls who only want to pound the keys,
call forth chords deep and sweet, a glissando
to slide out of danger just in time. I don't complete
the purchase, but it sits open in a tab. You could
have this, if you really needed it, I sing to
the frightened face of a younger self. No one
could say no. Together we could play for as long
as we want, until our melodies reintegrate.

Honeybells

I ordered a crate of tangerines for my future self. They arrived the first week of January, a bounty at my doorstep. My daughter grabs for them, straight out of the crate recognizing their brightness, the gleam of treasure.

Open it, open it! Peel under your nails, dig your fingers in! Tug apart the wedges of the fruit, spend out, taste it all now. Each bite is the solid smack of a catch in my palm. Now, now, don't wait!

The spray of juice leaves a scent that will cling to my fingers and lips long after we've eaten all the joy.

The Multiverse of the Pond

Two worlds split down the middle of the black water.
The wind doing heavy work
pockmarking the ice on the east side of the pond
thin and spider-cracked on the west.

More stories sleep underneath;
the potential for waking.
Who will find a home next season in the deep?
Who has always been here,
so small the shore of the water is a distant galaxy?

Which delicate side am I on,
the known drop or the unknown slide?
What's the next step where every choice is a risk?
Too many times I've flipped a coin and let chance
decide for me.

Will it be a good year for wood frogs
or will a blue heron visit
her spindly legs landing like the daggers of change?

I dither over cups of tea, inside as
a blizzard blankets the pond
under snow so deep it would appear
to be nothing more than an open field.
Foxes and turkeys cross the radius
unaware how, in the warm winter
of another universe,
the whiteness melts away
and they see their doppelganger,
before their feet get wet.

Either way, I will fall in the shock of cold
and wouldn't it have been better
to be in the bright, safe universe where I jumped?

IV. Until We Run Out

Xylophone

Snow melt from the roof into the gutter
clinks like the lower register of the oversized
wooden xylophone in the grass of the
art museum courtyard, a hands-on sensory
experience with rubber-tipped mallets wrapped
with blue painter's tape so they wouldn't
get lost among the piles of fallen apples.

They took the xylophone away when they had to hide
anything multiple people might touch. Still, they let
the apples fall. They littered the path, bites
taken out by kids who didn't know teeth marks
meant transmission; too young to have seen a
zombie movie or too safe to have learned about death.

13 Thoughts You Had in Rapid Succession When She Walked the Opposite Direction Down the Road

1. That's ok, I've been alone before. Not on this road, but another road.
2. (All roads)
3. I thought she was going to be the one to help me change that.
4. Her hair falls beautifully across her shoulders. The sun makes it look almost blue.
5. Is she too far away to hear me if I shout?
6. I can't make her name come out of my mouth. She's just getting further away.
7. Soon, something will hurt enough that it will replace this memory as the worst.
8. She's walking away. It still hurts. I need to start waking. Down my side. Further away.
9. I whisper her name. It will always come out a whisper from now on.
10. If I walk far enough down this road, it will circle back around the world and I will be facing her again. She will smile. His hair will look almost blue in the sun, crow feather iridescence.
11. She will smile when she sees me, the way she always did.
12. Soon, this won't hurt.
13. Soon.

10:11

The dark window separates
the white of an egg dripping
from the shell of the moon.

The water carves itself
a narrow channel within
the cone of the icicle.

Will you hold me like old guitar
you are trying to remember
how to play? Or the organ,

both hands on the keys
of my ribs, so that I might cry
with the song of release.

Shelterbelt

Against the gale of bad takes, and
scrolling chyrons, you ask me
to build you a windbreak, a
shelterbelt where we might hide.

Put a piece of leather around
the waist of safety, pull it taut. If you
cannot find cover, thrive in the eddy
made by the branches of my arms.

There is no straight line in this stream
of warnings and updates and subtweets,
no lake effect, to pause for reflection.
Only surface analysis, streamlined numbers.

We must secure our own survival,
root hope into the soil, make a home
there to withstand the perpendicular
onslaught of perpetual breaking news.

Superstition

Throw salt over your shoulder every time you use it, not just for a spill, so that you might go grain by grain toward your wish.

Leave a window open during a thunderstorm, to keep from being closed in.

Cover the injured mice wrenched from the cat jaws with a leaf or a flower in the underbrush.

Always leave more wildflowers than you pick, or they might decide not to grow back next year.

Count crows but not robins, lest you try to limit joy.

Don't open umbrellas in the house; I don't remember why.

Don't trim a forsythia bush until after all the yellow flowers fall; you should not shorten something already so brief.

Be careful: sorrow cannot be kept away by wish or ritual, but you may throw a rock in the other direction and run.

Mammalian Dive Reflex

A muscle twitches in my forehead, just above my eyebrow, as if I am about to scowl, over and over. You touch your finger to it and I remember when we were water-bound, floating, fingers twined and weeds caressing us, drawing us in. The boat was nearby, capsized, content as the canoe we had flipped on purpose, so anxious to get wet.

I squinted up at the hazy sun and that was maybe the body memory deep in the shape of my face, the water splashing over my hairline, where the rim of sunglasses would have sat, had I not lost them in the plunge.

Small fish come up to test whether we are food, and not yet, not while we still live, and float, and laugh as we are tickled by their quick fins.

I rest my head in my hands, remembering the pause before the decision to go back for the boat or swim to a stranger's dock looking for a skiff for a tow. On the creaky boards of wood worn grey lay a stiff musty towel that we would nevertheless use to wipe our eyes. We sat warming in the sun like the frogs that called from shore, knowing that we had to go back to clean up the mess, but finding it harder and harder to uncoil the rope of our limbs for the hard tug of reigning ourselves back in.

The Wrong Time to Ask Questions About a Rope Bridge Is When You're In the Middle

I don't mean the kind in ninja adventures for corporate team-building. I mean the ones in jungle adventure movies, or in dungeon crawls. Creaky, swaying over misty darkness below.

I'm not sure who put it there in the first place. How are rope bridges built in the first place? It's not something you can do half-way. Do you need to know how to fly? Can you suspend yourself, like the rope itself? Can you toss something so unwieldy across a chasm?

There are bats down there, probably, or one long, slithering something in the swampy water. There are boards missing. Some are ready to crumble to dust the moment any weight lands on them.

Once you get to the other side, you have to come back. Test your faith, your defiance of gravity, of the monster that lurks underneath.

Back and forth, the creak, the swing. What's worse, to topple off as the bridge still stretches across the rushing river, or to try to hang on as it snaps? Will you survive the wild swing, the crash into the rock wall? Can you climb what was once a horizontal curve of passage, now a ladder, which needs your arms?

Is the water below really that churning? That shockingly cold? Would you survive? Dodge the sharp rocks, come up for air?

Is the monster helpful? Friendly? Are they hungry for something that does not have wings?

The Disruption

Were I to launch myself into the pond,
I would get a face full of mud.

But first —
oh, but first —
clear cold water would shock me.

Ancient oak leaves and red maple
buds would caress my lips.
The frogs would scatter.

Constellations of skunk cabbage,
a mantle of forsythia. I would be marked
irrevocably as a disruptor.

My shadow across the water,
the pruned branches of memories
passed through generations of salamanders

who saw my hair, dripping wet,
as weeds upon which to lay their eggs.

For the Hopeless Scroll Under the Swipe of Your Finger

Do not succumb to despair.
The bakery is hiring,
which means tomorrow, someone
will be making bread.

The scent will travel across the canal,
and down the empty street in the early morning.
You will know it in your fragile inhalation.

And if we lose this now
we will find it again,
and we will make bread
until we run out of pans.

Previous Publications

'Some Mornings' appeared in *Impossible Archetype*, March 2020
'The Window' and 'Animate' appeared in *Feral Poetry*, June 2020
'The Disruption' appeared in *Stone of Madness*, September 2020
'The Five of Us (Are Saving Your Life)' appeared in *perhappened*, September 2020
'The Blade' appeared in *Serotonin*, October 2020
'Sam Peabody' appeared in *Windows Facing Windows*, November 2020
'Tender Cherie' appeared in *Agapanthus*, December 2020
'Paquerette' and 'Simple Ritual' appeared in *Feral Poetry*, December 2020
'For the Hopeless Scroll under the Swipe of Your Finger' appeared in *Pages Penned in Pandemic*, January 2021
'Audiation' appeared in Kalopsia, February, 2021

Acknowledgments

Thank you to Wyn and Lindsey for helping shape these poems. Thank you to Amanda, Elisabeth, Beth, and everyone at Animal Heart Press for bringing this chapbook together. Thank you to Ollie for the aspirational space geese. Thank you to all the independent magazine editors and creators for including my work in your publications and keeping the poetry scene vibrant and accessible.

About the Author

Jerica Taylor is a non-binary neurodivergent queer cook, birder, and chicken herder. She has an MFA from Emerson College. Winner of the Tiran Burrell Prize, their chapbook *Eyes, My Darling* will be released with Knight's Library in October 2022. Their prose chapbook *Donuts in Space*, about a stress baker aboard a spaceship, is available from GASHER Press. She lives with her wife and young daughter in Western Massachusetts. You can find them on Twitter @jericatruly and at jericataylor.com.

www.ingramcontent.com/pod-product-compliance
Lightning Source LLC
Chambersburg PA
CBHW060220050426
42446CB00013B/3126